When Pigs Fly

A Bible Memory Buddy® Book

Written by Mike Nappa
Illustrated by David Harrington

Loveland, Colorado
group.com/vbs

When Pigs Fly

Visit our websites: **4everybuddy.com**
group.com
group.com/vbs

When Pigs Fly is published in association with Nappaland Literary Agency, an independent agency dedicated to publishing works that are: Authentic. Relevant. Eternal. Visit us on the Web at NappalandLiterary.com.

ISBN 978-0-7644-8189-5
Printed in the United States of America
10 9 8 7 6 5 4 3 2 1   14 13 12

For Breezy & Bean, who always make me smile.

—MN

To my wonderful kids, Chase, Nick, and Emma.

—DH

Once upon a time, a—
Wait a minute...you are NOT a pig.

This story requires a pig. Hmm.

Fine. We'll get Orville to play the pig. Can you at least help out with sound effects?

Let's hear "Happy Pig"...How about "Sad Pig"?

OK, you'll do. Now, where were we? Ah, yes...

Once upon a time,
Away upon a dream,
There was a faithful pig
Named Orville St. McLean.

Orville could do lots of things, like
Painting pink car-nations.

Plus he always was the best at football imitations.

Ahem. Orville? *Football imitations.*

But one thing Orville couldn't do—
It sometimes made him cry—

He wished he could and wished it good,

But Orville couldn't fly.

(Psst. Do your "Sad Pig" sound effect now!)

Now Orville was a happy pig...

Ahem. *Happy Pig.*

Really? That's the best "Happy Pig" sound you can do? Let's try it again, with feeling this time:
Now Orville was a Happy Pig...

Better. OK, let's keep moving forward.

Now Orville was a happy pig.
He said a little prayer
That God would show him just how he
Could rocket through the air.

Orville and his friends asked God
For help and understanding

To find a piggy-perfect plan
For take-off and safe landing.

Orville? Hello?

Oh no....Our hero pig didn't know he was afraid of heights! Shake this book a bit, will you? Maybe that'll get him jump-started for take-off.

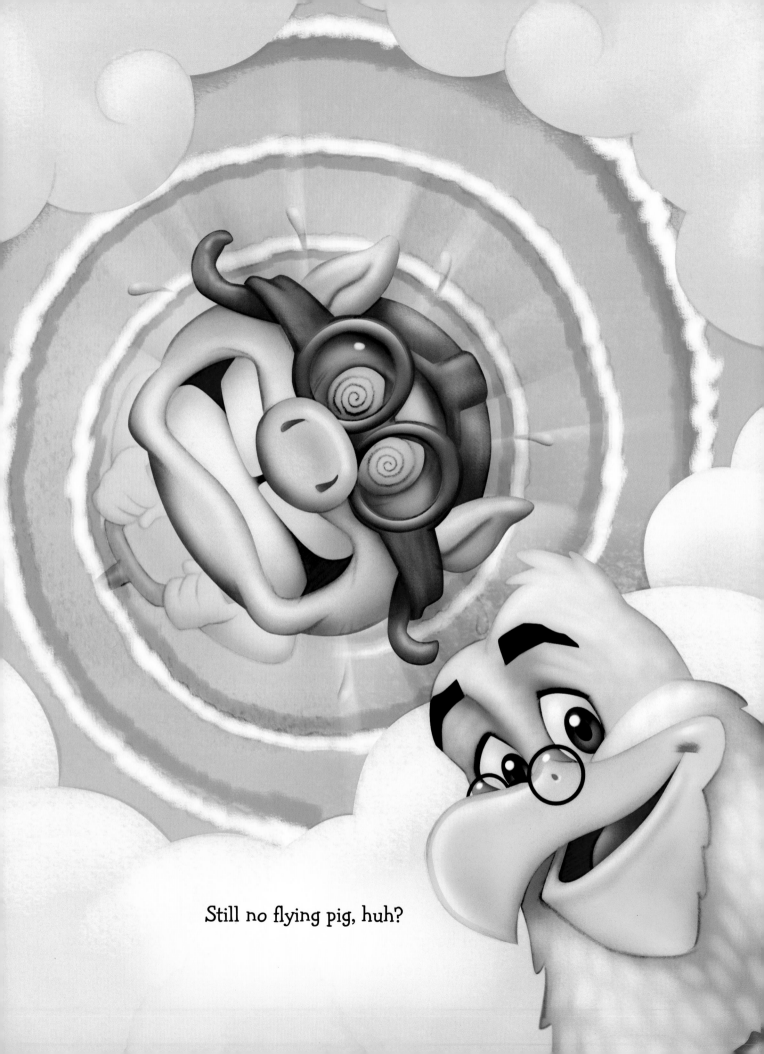

Still no flying pig, huh?

Maybe it'll help if you whisper encouragement into Orville's ear.
Let's get closer, and then you can remind him:
"It's possible with God!"

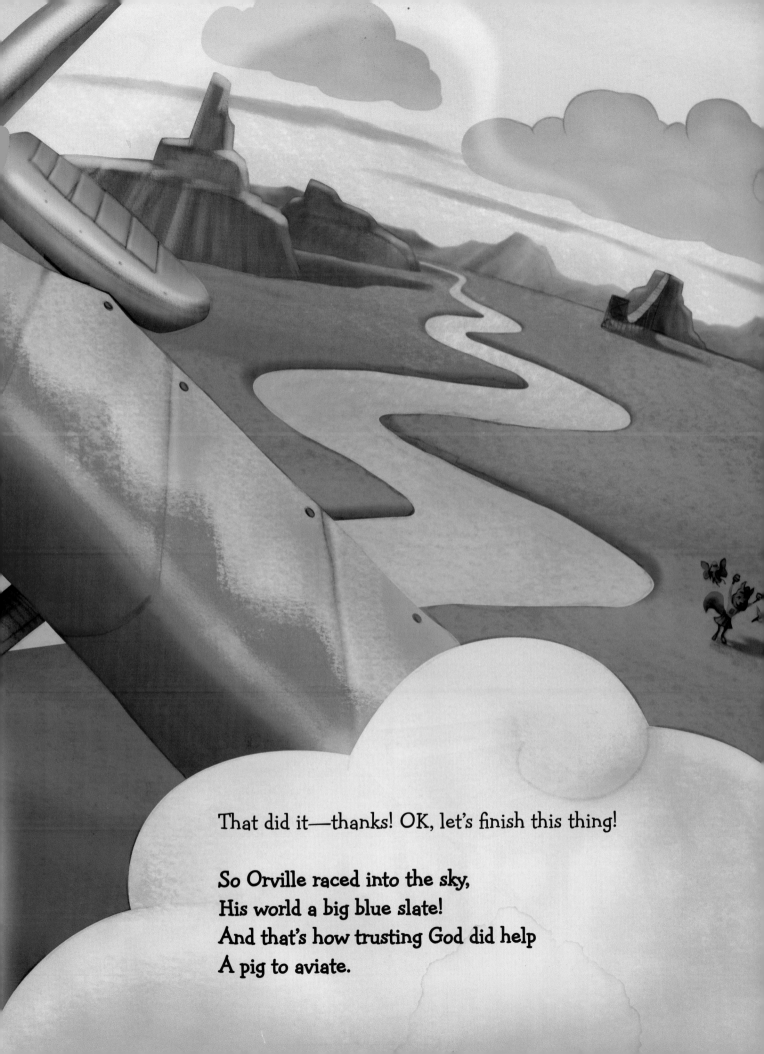

That did it—thanks! OK, let's finish this thing!

So Orville raced into the sky,
His world a big blue slate!
And that's how trusting God did help
A pig to aviate.

EVERYTHING IS POSSIBLE WITH GOD

MARK 10:27